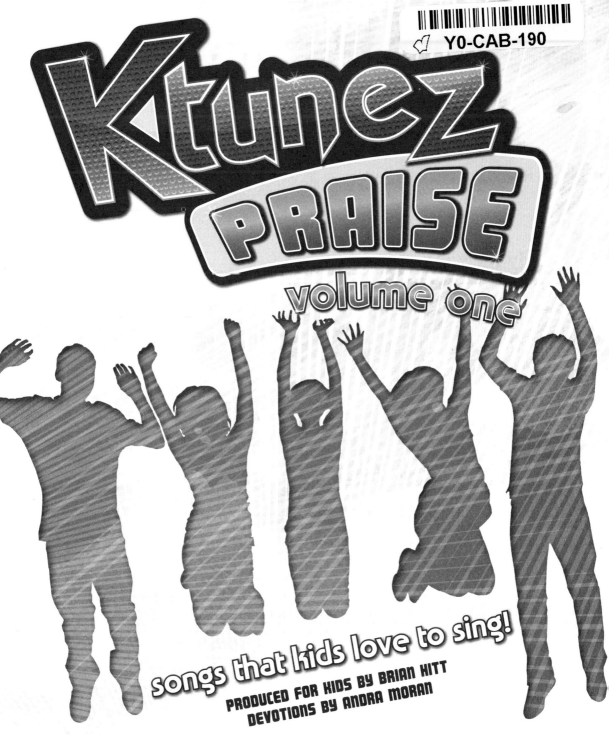

Ktunez PRAISE
volume one

songs that kids love to sing!

PRODUCED FOR KIDS BY BRIAN HITT
DEVOTIONS BY ANDRA MORAN

www.brentwoodbenson.com

 a division of  BRENTWOOD-BENSON
music publications

© MMXIII Brentwood-Benson Music Publications, 101 Winners Circle, Brentwood, TN 37027. All Rights Reserved. Unauthorized Duplication Prohibited.

DEVOTIONS INCLUDED FOR EVERY SONG!

Y0-CAB-190

CONTENTS

Ask God for Help
(Big Ol' Whale)

Words and Music by
BRIAN HITT and STEPHEN SHARP
Arranged by Brian Hitt

Bright Shuffle (♩=132)

CHOIR

There was a man named Jo-nah who did-n't want to do what God said. He tried_____ to run a-

© Copyright 2012 Universal Music - Brentwood Benson Songs / Dallas Street Publishing (BMI)
(Licensing through Music Services) / NYONKURO Music (Administered by Music Services). All rights reserved. Used by permission.
PLEASE NOTE: Copying of this music is NOT covered by the CCLI license. For CCLI information call 1-800-234-2446.

Ask God for Help (Big Ol' Whale)

Song Devotional

by Andra Moran

Let's think of the stinkiest places on earth: The locker room of a football team, the garbage cans behind a fried chicken restaurant, an old cheese factory...

What can you think of?

Well, those places might be the stinkiest places on earth, but how about the stinkiest place in an ocean? I'm willing to bet it's in the belly of a whale!

Just imagine: Jonah was in the belly of the whale with all of that stale saltwater and a pile of fish guts for three days and three nights! Ewwww! (Jonah 1:17).

Take a moment to read the next part of Jonah's story from the Bible. (Jonah 2:1-6)

Imagine how afraid Jonah must have felt! He probably thought he would be stuck inside the whale forever. Jonah did something very smart, though. During his scariest moment in the belly of the whale, he called out to God and asked for help!

We can learn a lot from Jonah's story, but the biggest lesson to remember today is that God is there to help you whenever you ask. This doesn't mean you'll always get the solution to your problem that you have in mind. But, you can be sure that God will always hear your prayer and lift you up out of whatever stinky situation you're in!

Why don't we stop and say a prayer right now?

God who made all creatures, great and small,

We thank You for hearing our little prayer today.

We are going to take a moment right now to silently think about a problem in our lives, and ask You to help us know what to do.

[silence is kept]

We know that You, Lord, are greater than even the biggest problems, and that we can always come to You for help. Thank you for being with us everywhere, even in the belly of a whale!

Amen.

Jesus Is the Only Way

Words and Music by
BRIAN HITT, BRENT BAXTER
and JAY SPEIGHT
Arranged by Brian Hitt

I could sail a boat or hold my breath and float to an ice-berg full of Es-ki-mos. I could ride a bike

© Copyright 2012 Universal Music - Brentwood Benson Songs / Dallas Street Publishing (BMI) (Licensing through Music Services) /
Hip Elephant Music (ASCAP) (Administered by Right Angle Music) / Cowboy Chords Music. All rights reserved. Used by permission.
PLEASE NOTE: Copying of this music is NOT covered by the CCLI license. For CCLI information call 1-800-234-2446.

Jesus Is the Only Way

Song Devotional

By Andra Moran

Have you ever heard of a homing pigeon? Homing pigeons are very interesting birds that are bred to be able to find their way home over long distances! Sometimes they are used to carry messages. They are very dependable messengers, because they only travel one way: home!

How good are you with directions?   Do you think you could find your way home from school? How about from church? How about finding your way home from outer space?

It's fun to imagine all the places we could go in our lives, like an iceberg near the home of the Eskimos, or off to college after the 7th grade, but no matter where we go, we always have a home to return to. Home has a special place in our hearts! Home is the place that we feel loved, treasured and known all the way to our core. Sounds like heaven, doesn't it?

Did you know that "home" is one of the oldest known names for God in the whole world? When you think about the many paths you might take in your life, think about the homing pigeon, always returning home. No matter where you go, remember that you are always to return to where your heart is: Home with Jesus! This home can be both in our hearts and in heaven with God!

In John 14, we can read Jesus' own words about being the way home to God! Take some time this week to read John 14 and think about what it means for Jesus to call Himself "The Way, The Truth and The Life."

Let's say a prayer together:

Dear God,

Today I want to thank You for giving me a life that is full of possibilities! I can go many places, but more than anywhere in the whole world, I want to be with You. Help me to stay on the path that You have for me. I know it is my only way. I love You, Jesus!

Amen.

My Body Is a Temple

Words and Music by
BRIAN HITT, BRENT BAXTER
and JAY SPEIGHT
Arranged by Brian Hitt

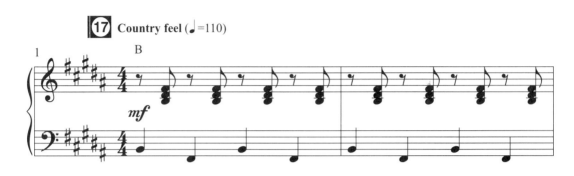

© Copyright 2012 Universal Music - Brentwood Benson Songs / Dallas Street Publishing (BMI)
(Licensing through Music Services) / Hip Elephant Music (ASCAP) (Administered by Right Angle Music) /
Writer's Infinity Music (Administered by Infinity Music Group). All rights reserved. Used by permission.
PLEASE NOTE: Copying of this music is NOT covered by the CCLI license. For CCLI information call 1-800-234-2446.

I can be a health-y kid like God wants me to be.

Chase the dog, hop like a frog, throw the ball till mom-ma calls me

— in. Yeah, my

bod - y is a tem - ple__ where my Friend, Je - sus,

My Body Is a Temple

Song Devotional

by Andra Moran

Can you describe the perfect home? Use your imagination! What would it look like?

Would there be a skateboard ramp from upstairs to downstairs? A high-dive and a swimming pool in the backyard? How about a garden with strawberry plants and tall trees for climbing? Would there be a special corner with big bean bag chairs to settle into for reading all your favorite books?

Speaking of books, did you know that there is a book in the Bible that says God has made us a home for the Holy Spirit? I Corinthians 6:19 calls our human bodies the home, or the temple, of the Holy Spirit. This verse reminds us how important our bodies are! After all, our bodies are pretty special if they are temples for the Holy Spirit!

This means that we must take good care of our bodies: stay healthy, clean, and cared for. Nobody would want to live in a dirty home filled with trash, right?

One way we can take care of our bodies is to eat right. What kind of food would you have in the refrigerator of the temple for the Holy Spirit? I bet it would be healthy, natural food and vegetables so that you can grow strong bones and live a long, happy life!

The Bible even says something about food! Genesis 1:29 reads, "God said, 'I give you every seed-bearing plant on the face of the whole earth, and every tree that has fruit with seed in it. They will be yours for food.'" Fortunately, God has given us a bunch of delicious food options that grow right out of the earth to keep our bodies healthy, happy and strong!

Take a few minutes to think about things you can do to make your body healthy so that it is a happy home for the Holy Spirit to live in. Eating your vegetables, washing all the dirt of playtime off, and playing outside are all good choices to make.

Let's say a prayer together.

Dear Jesus,

We want to be happy homes for You! We were made by You, and we belong to You, Lord. We know You live in us. Help us to make good choices with our bodies so that we can honor You.

Amen.

VIP

Words and Music by
BRIAN HITT
and MICHAEL FORDINAL
Arranged by Brian Hitt

© Copyright 2012 Universal Music - Brentwood Benson Songs / Dallas Street Publishing (BMI).
(Licensing through Music Services) / Songs For the Deer (BMI). All rights reserved. Used by permission.
PLEASE NOTE: Copying of this music is NOT covered by the CCLI license. For CCLI information call 1-800-234-2446.

VIP

Song Devotional

by Andra Moran

I've got an idea. Picture a person you know well… someone you love very much. Now, in the picture you have in your mind, zoom in on that person's hair. Got a good clear picture of that hair? Great! Now, answer this: How many hairs are there on that person's head?

What do you mean you don't know? This is a person you know really well! Someone you love! And you don't even know how many hairs they have?

Of course, I'm kidding a little bit. It is nearly impossible for human beings to be able to count the number of hairs on another person's head. But the Bible reminds us over and over that nothing is impossible with God! (Luke 18:27)

God knows each one of us so well that he knows the number of hairs on our head and every thought in our minds! (Matthew 10:30) God knows our hearts and emotions whether we are happy or excited or angry or sad.

God knows us and loves us. We are important to God – very important! God cares about us so much! We are all God's VIPs – very important people! We are children of the King of kings!

Sometimes it is easy to think that we don't matter to anyone. In these times, you might want to say this little prayer:

Dear God,

Thank you so much for believing that I am a very important person. My heart beats with joy to know that You treasure me. I want to be a VIP for You, and share Your love with every heart and soul that I meet.

Amen.

Everybody Needs Jesus

Words and Music by
BRIAN HITT, BRENT BAXTER
and JAY SPEIGHT
Arranged by Brian Hitt

Rid-ers on the sub-way, pi-lots in an air-plane, ba-bies in the

© Copyright 2012 Universal Music - Brentwood Benson Songs / Dallas Street Publishing (BMI)
(Licensing through Music Services) / Hip Elephant Music (ASCAP) (Administered by Right Angle Music) / Writer's Infinity Music
(Administered by Infinity Music Group). All rights reserved. Used by permission.
PLEASE NOTE: Copying of this music is NOT covered by the CCLI license. For CCLI information call 1-800-234-2446.

40

44

Everybody Needs Jesus

Song Devotional

by Andra Moran

If you think about it, the word "everybody" is really funny. It's funny because it lumps all kinds of different people together. You might notice that many people tend to be friends with others who think like they do, or who have the same interests, or like the same things. But, did you know that everybody has one thing in common?

Whether you're a clown or a cowboy, a heavyweight wrestler or a movie director, everybody needs Jesus!

We need Jesus to light up our lives and save us from the darkness of sin and sadness.

Did you know that in the Bible, Jesus is called the Light of the World? (John 8:12)

This is a great name for Jesus, because when the sun is shining, it shines on everybody at the same time! Nobody is left out! Everybody is covered by the light of the Son of God.

In the eighth chapter of John, Jesus says, "I am the light of the world! Whoever follows me will never walk in darkness, but will have the light of life."

We all have the same invitation to follow Jesus, and to walk in the light. Astronauts, babies, sailors, tightrope walkers, rock stars, your neighbors, your friends at school – everybody!

How will people hear about Jesus' invitation? Well, that part is up to us.

We get to share the Good News by telling those around us. Soon everyone will know about Jesus' love for all of us!

Let's pray:

Jesus, Light of the World,

We need You! We need Your light to cover our world, casting out any darkness. Let us shine as bright examples of how You want us to live, sharing Your love with everybody we meet. Thank You, Jesus!

Amen.

Smile

Words and Music by
BRIAN HITT and MICHAEL FARREN
Arranged by Brian Hitt

40 **Syncopated Latin feel** (♩=118)

CHOIR

There's a love that won't bend or __ break,

the kind of hug that you can't es - cape.

© Copyright 2012 Universal Music - Brentwood Benson Songs / Dallas Street Publishing (BMI) (Licensing through Music Services) / Farren Love and War Publishing (Administered by Word Music, LLC) / Word Music, LLC. All rights reserved. Used by permission.
PLEASE NOTE: Copying of this music is NOT covered by the CCLI license. For CCLI information call 1-800-234-2446.

Smile

Song Devotional

by Andra Moran

Who wants to play a game? Let's play Simon Says! Ready?

Simon Says: Put your hands on your head.

Simon Says: Touch your toes.

Simon Says: Jump three times.

Simon Says: Say "Cheese!"

I can't hear you! I said, say "Cheese!"

Gotcha! I made you smile!

You know, we have a lot of opportunities to smile in our lives! A good grade in school, a funny story that makes you laugh, a Christmas present you were really hoping for, special time with family and friends, a beautiful sunny day...

All of these things bring smiles to our faces, but the love of God brings a smile to our souls!

You can't really see or touch your soul, but you can feel it when your soul is smiling. When our souls smile, it feels even better than happiness! Maybe you can imagine this feeling as pure joy bubbling through all of your veins – making you laugh and making you smile!

It sure makes me have a big smile of joy to know that God's love is forever! It won't bend, it won't break, it won't be angry or mean, no matter what! God's love is the real deal.

There are four places in the Bible where we read this very special instruction from God: "Love the LORD your God with all your heart, all your mind and all your soul." (Deuteronomy 6:5, Joshua 22:5, Matthew 22:37, Luke 10:27)

God wants us to love Him, because He loves us so much!

You know what? I bet God smiles when He hears us say that we love Him! So let's say it in a prayer:

Dear God,

We love You with all our hearts, all our minds, and all our souls. We hope You can feel us smiling at You today.

Amen.

L-O-V-E U God

Words and Music by
BRIAN HITT and JASON COX
Arranged by Brian Hitt

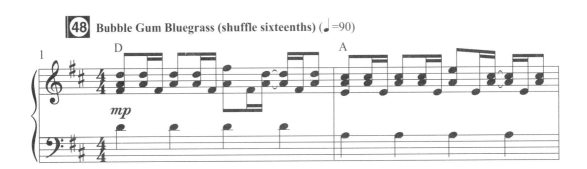

© Copyright 2012 Universal Music - Brentwood Benson Songs / Dallas Street Publishing (BMI)
(Licensing through Music Services) / Cox Rox Music. All rights reserved. Used by permission.
PLEASE NOTE: Copying of this music is NOT covered by the CCLI license. For CCLI information call 1-800-234-2446.

62

L - O, L-O - V-E You, God.

Hey,— oh!

L-O-V-E U God

Song Devotional

By Andra Moran

Do you know what "warm fuzzies" are? Warm fuzzies are the happy feelings that we have when we feel love! It sure is nice to think about how we are loved, isn't it? On the count of three, see if you can feel a warm fuzzy by naming five people who love you. Ready? One, two, three, GO!

That is a fun list to make, isn't it?

You know, warm fuzzies don't just come to us when we get love. We also get warm fuzzies when we give love! So now, let's make a list of five people that you love, and feel another warm fuzzy. Ready? One, two, three, GO!

We must always remember that God and Jesus and the Holy Spirit are on both warm fuzzy lists: The list of who loves us, and the list of who we love! Now here's a question for you: What are some ways we can share warm fuzzies with God?

There are lots of ways to answer this question! One of my favorites is to sing praises to God. Psalm 147:1 says, "Praise the LORD. How good it is to sing praises to our God, how pleasant and fitting to praise him!"

Singing praises to God makes us feel gladness, joy and warm fuzzies, because God is worthy of our praise!

Let's pray:

Holy God,

You make the world spin around, the sun shine and the rain fall. You are all around us and in the very breath we breathe. We worship You, O God, because, God, You do all of this with great love for us! We L-O-V-E You, God.

Amen.

Bigger Than Me

Words and Music by
BRIAN HITT and JAY SPEIGHT
Arranged by Brian Hitt

Lyrics: I may nev-er know what to-mor-row holds, but I know You have a _____ plan.

© Copyright 2012 Universal Music - Brentwood Benson Songs / Dallas Street Publishing (BMI) (Licensing through Music Services) / Hip Elephant Music (ASCAP) (Administered by Right Angle Music). All rights reserved. Used by permission.
PLEASE NOTE: Copying of this music is NOT covered by the CCLI license. For CCLI information call 1-800-234-2446.

Bigger Than Me

Song Devotional

By Andra Moran

How tall are you? Do you know?

Carefully put your hand on top of your head. Then, move your hand slowly away from your head and in a straight line in front of you. Let your eyes look up at your hand without moving. Now, keep still and let your eyes look to the ground.

See that?

That's how tall you are. Tallness is one of the ways we humans measure how big we are.

Now, think about God. God is *so* big! God is bigger than all things! God is strong, too! God is stronger than any storm that may blow into our lives. And do you know my favorite thing about God? It's that we can always count on God to be good and to love us.

Psalm 100:5 puts it this way: "For the Lord is good, and his love endures forever. His faithfulness continues through all generations."

Over and over, the Bible tells us that we can rely on God to stay with us and to love us, steadfast and true, forever and ever. From the littlest baby to the oldest grandma, God is strong, faithful and good!

So, whether you are big or small, you can always count on God to be there for you with a big, big love that is bigger than you can ever imagine!

Let's pray!

Dear God,

Help us to remember that Your big, big love surrounds us always! From small to tall, You love us all, and that is something to celebrate.

Amen.

Give God the Glory

Words and Music by
BRIAN HITT and APRIL GEESBREGHT
Arranged by Brian Hitt

© Copyright 2012 Universal Music - Brentwood Benson Songs / Dallas Street Publishing (BMI) (Licensing through Music Services) /
Sony/ATV Music Publishing LLC / Chatterbox Music. All rights on behalf of Sony/ATV Music Publishing LLC /
Chatterbox Music administered by Sony/ATV Music Publishing LLC (8 Music Square West, Nashville, TN 37203).
International copyright secured. All rights reserved. Used by permission. Reprinted by permission of Hal Leonard Corporation.
PLEASE NOTE: Copying of this music is NOT covered by the CCLI license. For CCLI information call 1-800-234-2446.

Give God the Glory

Song Devotional

by Andra Moran

What does it mean when someone says, "That's the icing on the cake!" Do you know?

You're right! It means that there is something good that's topped with something extra good.

In this song, we have a lot of things that are good together. Can you name some? Let's give it a try together.

Song and words, castle and king, bell and ring… You did it!

Want to know another pair that's great together? God and us!

The Bible tells us that whatever we do, we should do it in the name of the Lord, Jesus! (Colossians 3:17) One reason for this is because Jesus is always with us! (Matthew 28:20).

Having a friend like Jesus means we are never alone. Jesus is right there with us when we sing, when we dance, when we pray, when we rock out on the electric guitar. Now that is something to celebrate! We give God the glory and we praise His name for all the wonderful ways He loves us and knows our hearts. We give God the glory because God is truly great! His everlasting love is the icing on our cake!

Let's pray together:

Holy God,

We want to live our lives in a way that gives You glory and praise. We ask You to help us stay mindful of Your presence and remind us to stay connected to You in every thing we say and do.

Amen.

Thank You

Words and Music by
BRIAN HITT and MICHAEL FARREN
Arranged by Brian Hitt

© Copyright 2012 Universal Music - Brentwood Benson Songs / Dallas Street Publishing (BMI) (Licensing through Music Services) / Farren Love and War Publishing (Administered by Word Music, LLC) / Word Music, LLC. All rights reserved. Used by permission.
PLEASE NOTE: Copying of this music is NOT covered by the CCLI license. For CCLI information call 1-800-234-2446.

Thank You

Song Devotional

by Andra Moran

Stand up as tall as you can, and stretch your arms out wide, as far apart as possible. Now, turn your head from side to side, and look at your hands. Can you see the distance between them?

Now, imagine that you had a great big piece of paper between your hands. Let's pretend to fold that paper in half. Now, what do you have? A card, that's right!

One thing that is very nice to do when you have been given a gift is to make a thank you card to send to the person who gave you the present.

Now, think about that big card we just imagined. Even a card that big wouldn't be big enough to say "Thank You" to Jesus for the gift that He gave us when He died on the cross for us!

The amazing thing about the gift Jesus gave us is that He gave it to us freely! His gift was a perfect sacrifice of love and we didn't do anything to deserve it! Jesus gave us the gift of His life because He loves us. We are saved by grace. In the book of Ephesians in the Bible, Paul writes, "For it is by grace that you are saved, through faith, and this is not from yourselves. It is the gift of God!" (Ephesians 2:8)

When we talk with Jesus in our prayers, we can thank Jesus for His love, and tell Him that we love Him, too! We can live our lives in a way that shows Jesus that we want to give a gift back to Him: The gift of living in a way that honors Jesus!

Let's talk to Jesus now, okay?

Dear Jesus,

We come before You with open arms and open hearts to say "Thank You" for the gift of Your life. We want to offer our lives back to You, too. Surround us with a sense of Your presence always, and remind us that it is by grace that we are saved. We know we could never pay back Your gift, so help us to always be grateful for the gift of Your love.

Amen.

essential KIDZ
Resource DVD

A FUN
Resource to enhance your kids' worship serivce!

CALL TODAY FOR A FREE DVD SAMPLER!

essential **KIDZ**
A Fun DVD Resource for Kidz Worship

This DVD resource includes:

- Praise & Worship - 8 great songs with exciting visuals and onscreen lyrics. Songs include: *Big House, King of the Jungle, His Cheeseburger, Every Move I Make* and more

- Count Downs - 2 visual count downs to let your kids know when service begins.

- Birthday Songs – 2 new fun birthday songs with full-mix and split trax options.

- Segment Title Screens - Includes: Praise & Worship, Game Time, Tithes & Offerings, Memory Verse, Prayer Time, Quiet Time, and Story Time.

Call **Brentwood-Benson** today
at **1-800-846-7664**
or visit us on line at
www.BrentwoodBenson.com